Instead of Whom
Does the Flower Bloom

THE POEMS OF VLADO KRESLIN

essential translations series 6

Instead of Whom
Does the Flower Bloom

THE POEMS OF VLADO KRESLIN

Translated by Urška Charney

GUERNICA

TORONTO – BUFFALO – BERKELEY – LANCASTER (U.K.) 2012

Copyright © 1991, Vlado Kreslin and Založba M&M
Original title: *Namesto koga roža cveti*

Copyright © 2012, Urška Charney and Guernica Editions Inc.

Michael Mirolla, editor
Guernica Editions Inc.
P.O. Box 117, Station P, Toronto (ON), Canada M5S 2S6
2250 Military Road, Tonawanda, N.Y. 14150-6000 U.S.A.

Distributors:
University of Toronto Press Distribution,
5201 Dufferin Street, Toronto (ON), Canada M3H 5T8
Gazelle Book Services, White Cross Mills, High
Town, Lancaster LA1 4XS U.K.
Small Press Distribution, 1341 Seventh St.,
Berkeley, CA 94710-1409 U.S.A.

First edition.
Printed in Canada.

Legal Deposit – Third Quarter
Library of Congress Catalog Card Number: 2012938360

Library and Archives Canada Cataloguing in Publication

Kreslin, Vlado, 1953-
Instead of whom does the flower bloom : selected poems of
Vlado Kreslin / Vlado Kreslin ; Urska Charney, translator.

(Essential translations ; 6)
Translation of: Namesto koga roža cveti.
Also issued in electronic format.
ISBN 978-1-55071-636-8

Kreslin, Vlado, 1953- --Translations into English.
I. Charney, Urska II. Title. III. Series: Essential translations
(Toronto, Ont.) ; 6

PG1920.21.R38A6 2012   891.8'416   C2012-902922-X

CONTENTS

INTRODUCTION

Since we had a marvelous Slovenian musician
with us who performed during our readings and
who carried his guitar wherever he went, he and
a couple of others started singing Bosnian songs
during dinner, which they continued back at the
hotel late into the night, broadening their repertory
to Serbian, Hungarian, and Russian songs. Despite
all the bad blood and suspicion between them, the
various ethnic groups in that part of the world like
each other's music.

– Charles Simic in *The New York*
Review of Books (August 2011)

The mists part over a slow, green river that bends past an ancient mill, its wood weathered to the colour of ash. A stork crosses the sky, and strains of laughter and gypsy guitar waft downstream. This is Prekmurje, the land of Vlado Kreslin. It is the poorest, most remote region of Slovenia, tucked away beside the Hungarian border. It is a flat wetland dotted with low-slung farmhouses capped by stork nests. It is to Slovenia what Ireland long was to England – a land of quiet pride, beauty, and poverty. A land of poets.

There is no contemporary Slovenian poet who better embodies his homeland than Vlado Kreslin. In addition to his poetic success, he is even better known as one of the Balkan's most beloved folk rock musicians. Kreslin's thirty-year career has spanned performances with R.E.M.

and Bob Dylan, for whom he opened twice, and concerts around the world.

Vlado Kreslin is a national institution in Slovenia, having achieved the status of folk hero. Songs from his 14 albums, and based on his published poetry, have inspired films and novels. Kreslin has become a spokesperson and rainmaker for the renewed interest in not only Slovene music, but Balkan music in general. He toured refugee camps with a group of teenage refugee musicians during the war in Bosnia, and performed *sevdalinkas*, Bosnian love songs, at a concert in post-war Sarajevo – a dramatic enterprise, after the fighting of the Balkan War had so recently ended. Soon after the war, in December of 2000, Kreslin performed at another historic concert in Sarajevo, still talked about by those who attended. The concert featured artists from various factions that had so recently been at loggerheads, united on the same stage in a show of post-war solidarity. The poet and critic Charles Simic described Kreslin in the quotation that began this essay, when the two of them traveled through Bosnia during the 2011 "Sarajevo Days of Poetry." Kreslin's music, as with his poetry, helps rival nations and ethnic groups set aside the bad blood and suspicion between them, providing a joyous and emotional point of unification. Everyone can agree on the transcendental power of words and music.

The gospel that Kreslin preaches is unity through music and poetry. Yet he does not preach. His poems are, at least on the surface, apolitical. It is the pastoral imagery and accompanying music that intertwine elements from various antagonistic nations and ethnic groups into one work of art. This is embodied in many of his poems, such as "Black Guitar," which tell tales of Prekmurje, where Slovenes and gypsies live side-by-side, bound by the land and by their love for music.

Kreslin grew up in Prekmurje, where his grandfather ran a restaurant that included a performance space, where every weekend local musicians would gather and perform

– musicians who, thirty years later, Kreslin would perform with regularly in his own band. Both of his parents are singers themselves (indeed they still perform with him) and his childhood was surrounded by a festive atmosphere infused with music. Local musicians would perform for guests and for their own enjoyment long into the night, and Kreslin recalls frequently falling asleep as a child to the drone of violins and the thump and slap of the double bass that shook his bedroom wall.

Talented in languages, Kreslin studied first in the 1970s to be an English teacher, but his love was always music. He performed in a number of bands through the 1980s, including Martin Krpan (named after a legendary strongman of Slovenian folklore). Kreslin's innate charisma and nuanced voice made him a natural front man for these bands. An avid poet, he wrote the lyrics and co-wrote the music, while playing guitar and singing lead vocals. Some of the poems included in this collection began as lyrics to songs performed by Martin Krpan, including "Still Time" and "Vertiginous from the Height," which are still hugely popular in Slovenia, the latter being the premier love song in the Slovenian canon. I recommend listening to Kreslin's music after reading the poems in translation, to hear their nuances and the interpretation by Kreslin, who is a consummate actor as well as creator. The poems, as lyrics, take on a new meaning when performed with music, much as a play is fascinating to read, but benefits from the interpretation of an actor.

It was after Martin Krpan, when Kreslin set off on his own, that he truly emerged as an artist. He began to perform with some of the musicians who had played at his grandfather's restaurant in his youth, in the Prekmurje village of Beltinci. They formed what became known as Beltinška Banda (the Band of Beltinci), and some still played with Kreslin, even into their 80s. A beloved bass player, Joužek, passed away only recently (he performed until age 95), and received a beautiful poem, which became a favourite elegiac song, included in this collection, entitled "Joužek." Kreslin also encourages young musicians, and his new band was dubbed Mali Bogovi (Minor Gods). Seeing Kreslin perform on stage is a union of eras. Beltinska Banda plays alongside Mali Bogovi, octogenarians beside twenty-somethings. Their musicianship is without question but the tie that binds them is Kreslin the vocalist and writer, the bridge between generations, unifier of the sometimes antagonistic relationship between Slovenes and gypsies, and as mentioned before, unifier of the sometime warring factions in the southern Balkans, performing as he does with musicians from so many nations and ethnic groups within the former Yugoslavia.

Kreslin has been variously compared to several other musician/poets, 20th century troubadours, including Bob Dylan, Bruce Springsteen, and Woody Guthrie. Although it may not be fair to compare figures from such vastly different market sizes, the cultural and popular impact within a country of origin is equivalent and apt. Like Dylan, Kreslin has published books of lyrics and books of poetry, and other artists have been inspired by his work, including the title poem of this collection, which was the seed for both an award-winning novel, *Namesto koga roža cveti* by Feri Laišek (1991) and a well-received film, *Halgato*, directed by Andrej Mlakar (1995). Like Springsteen, Kreslin spans generations, performing with older folk musicians as well as young prodigies, and combining traditional regional music and folktales with his own original compositions. Like Guthrie, Kreslin is not merely a troubadour, but has become a folk symbol himself. Kreslin empowered the people of Prekmurje to take pride in speaking their own dialect and in their local cultural traditions. Kreslin is seen by some as a sort of spirit of Prekmurje. He is somewhere between Springsteen, adopted as the embodiment of a Romanticized ideal of New Jersey, and Woody Guthrie, as a spokesperson for the marginalized in America in the 30s and 40s.

Kreslin's poetry is a beautiful aesthetic experience, evocative and subtle, particularly rich in natural imagery. There are clear themes that run like veins throughout it: the Mura River (which winds through Prekmurje), the ubiquitous storks of Prekmurje and other avian images, an appreciation for gypsy culture (particularly their musical traditions), trans-generational and trans-cultural inspiration, mist and stars. One might imagine the poems best read in the early morning hours, on the mist-spread banks of the Mura.

These themes link the poems in this collection, which form an organic unit. Some are love stories, some folk tales, some are politically-driven. But those with a political bent are subtle enough that their meanings will likely evade readers who are not from Slovenia. They do not require an exegesis in order to be appreciated (the publisher determined that annotations would not be necessary in this volume, and I would agree), but there is more to them than meets the eye.

For example, the poem "Light the Day" is about the nation's state of mind when the present Prime Minister of Slovenia was imprisoned by the Yugoslav Army during the end of Socialism. "We Could Fly Away," which reads like a love poem, is actually about the temporary reconciliation after the Second World War of the liberals and the Christian Conservatives, two parties once more at odds with one another. "Fall in Anger" is about how those who became exemplary leaders and media opinion-makers after the end of Socialism were the same people who were schoolyard bullies and tattle-tales, and how they continue to employ the same tactics now that they hold office. "See, As the Train Winds On" is about the Slovene residents of the Veneto who were forcibly deported by Mussolini in order to toil in Belgian mines.

These undercurrents and references are not requisite to the appreciation of the poems, but it is worth mentioning that, although subtle, they are present.

In 2007 my wife and I wrote to Vlado Kreslin, simply to say that we were great fans of his music, and to ask if I might interview him for a magazine article. My wife is Slovenian, and I had been introduced to Kreslin's music by Slovenian friends. To our great surprise, Kreslin wrote back personally. I had somehow imagined that any major star would be surrounded by an entourage of "handlers" who would respond to emails on his behalf. But Kreslin is down-to-earth, a fan's dream. He once performed a private show for a fan from Texas who flew to Slovenia to see him perform, but who had arrived too late to see the real concert. We quickly became friends, my wife, the translator Urška Charney, and Vlado and his wife, Eva Strmljan Kreslin. This translation project came about through that friendship.

This book is one of two translations by Urška Charney to be published simultaneously by Guernica Editions. The other is a contemporary novel, a number one best-seller in Slovenia, *Zlati Dež* (*The Golden Shower*) by Luka Novak. They are Ms. Charney's first long-form translations from Slovenian into English, and demonstrate the exceptional breadth of her talent as a translator, able to handle both the modern, slang-filled prose of a literary novel and the subtle bounty of traditional poetry. This is all the more impressive because Ms. Charney never studied to be a translator. Her degrees are in comparative linguistics and sinology. While a student of languages, her translation abilities seem to have evolved organically, and it is with pride that I write this introduction to a book of poems written by a friend, and translated by my wife, both of whose work I admire greatly.

Vlado Kreslin was invited to Yale University in April 2009 by Professor Harvey Goldblatt of the Slavic Studies Department. As an honored guest, Kreslin gave an exclusive Master's Tea, performed a large concert and poetry reading, and was given the honorary title of Quincy Porter Fellow. In the same year, Kreslin was selected by the

Slovenian Ministry of Culture to tour Russia, Poland, and the Ukraine as an ambassador of Slovenian culture: poetry readings as a pan-Slavic bridge-building effort. With a cavalcade of awards and honors, as well as a new poetry collection that came out in Slovene in 2009 (*Pojezije* or *Sung Poems*, published by Založba Kreslin), now is an ideal time to introduce the poetry of Vlado Kreslin to an English-language readership.

With Kreslin's Yale visit, it became clear that while Kreslin's work is internationally renowned in both popular and academic circles, he remains little known outside of the Balkans and the ethnic Balkan communities abroad. This is largely because there is no translation of his work into English, save for a small print-run compilation of poetry-as-a-language-teaching-aide, currently out of print. Publications in 2011 of selected poems included here in prestigious literary journals, including *Confrontations*, *Erbacce*, and *Modern Poetry in Translation* further underscore the interest in Kreslin's work, and the skill of the translation by Urška Charney.

There has long been a strong interest in Balkan literature. But with the recent interest in Slovene culture, thanks to Slovenia's 2008 EU presidency, the 2011 designation of the Slovene city of Maribor as European Capital of Culture, coupled with Kreslin's honors at Yale University and as an ambassador of poetry for the Slovene Ministry of Culture, it is an ideal time to introduce the anglophone readership to the writings of this Slovene icon.

Enjoy this wonderful collection, which I hope will inspire you to visit Slovenia yourself. In the meantime, this book will transport you there.

Noah Charney
Ljubljana, Slovenia

Joužek

Year 1918,
The rifles drown in silence,
Slim fingers stroke the taut strings.
Age fourteen, dominated by numbness,
Away into a musician's night,
They play over morning melt of dew.

His fingers are versed to trace
The tears of joy and sorrow.
Those of a king, a beggar,
A bride or an idler.
These silky hands of a child
Imbued with his name.

To the feasts and gatherings,
And into the white world,
Here to priests,
And there to inebriated poets.
Even yesterday,
Together they kept time,
But today only his gnarled fingers
Play in a solitude reminiscent of yesterday.

His fingers are versed to trace
The tears of joy and sorrow.
Those of a king, a beggar,
A bride or an idler.
These old gnarled hands,
Imbued with a child's name.

Your gnarled hands, your double bass,
And a child's name,
Joužek, wait for me
There at your horizon.

It Is Not The Way Of Things

Under our sun this can't be done,
It is not the way of things
That a tree should blossom
And grow strong into the sky.

We don't venture off to heavens,
Instead we prefer to keep at home.
For the land of aliens might shatter
That highly thought-of image of our selves.

Safely sheltered by our beaten tracks,
On firm ground, doors always opened for us,
One good turn deserves another,
Herein begins the merry dance of brotherhood.

Same blood defines our unity,
Only familiar faces around us,
One good turn deserves another,
Nothing's as beautiful as home.

Under our sun this can't be done,
It is not the way of things
That a tree would blossom
And grow strong into the sky.

Here we stand to pull together,
To cut down the tree in prosperity,
Undergrowth and underbrush holding sway,
We form the forests' mighty plurality.

Generation

I loved to tread the earth alone,
The never-ending paths
That flew me to the stars.
My soul and I,
No other was king to my world.

Eager to find the truth in my heart,
I loved to eye a flower bud,
Neither colourful nor yet lush.

I loved to watch you go,
As though you were sent from god,
As though you were made of mud and gold.

Every time the sun
Disappears into an invisible horizon,
It runs the day over with night,
Shows its undeniable power.
It counts to five, counts to six,
Only two of us remain,
Here my generation
Comes to an end.

For one luminously starry night
I'd exchange a five star hotel,
For a joint or two
Under the welkin of Amsterdam.

Every time an innocent boy
Hides deep into a man,
He shatters and mends
The toys for them both.
He counts to five, counts to six,
Only two of us remain,
Here my generation
Comes to an end.

One Would Wish

We all strive to spend our time
Blemish free and pure.
Time wrapped in double laughter,
Aloud, harmonious and upright.

Without ailments and mortification,
Without anguish before the light of day,
Without eyes shut from truth.

We all wish to walk the path of life
With strides elegant and smooth.
With no steps which stagger heavy,
Always knowing
From and where we'll be led.

If only our eyes could speak straight from the heart,
Holding the right to paint pale cheeks red
Without hiding nor feigning ignorance,
If only we could be what we are.

We all yearn to stop time sometimes,
To make the world a better place,
To caress a flower's fugitive blossom
In pace slow and silent.

We all move towards
The single vanishing point, in perspective
We've disappeared beyond the horizon.
Like us,
The sun shrinks to nothingness,
Once set deep into darkness.

Minor Gods

Minor gods grow ever more minor.
Feigned, they profess to all believe in God.
The Commune of minor gods resounds louder,
Its echo thundering in the heavenly sky.

Even the most devout, now and then,
Find their souls roam the wavering paths of doubt,
For minor gods give their word,
New perspectives,
And the right ways.

Haughty and hollow they bounce
Up into high heaven.
They hear nothing
Under the deafening weights of pressure.
Elongated bloodthirsty fingers,
Deceiving squint-eyed,
Minor gods
See only what they wish to see.

Minor gods grow ever more minor!
Feigned, they profess to all believe in God.
Minor gods' intent voice resounds louder,
Their echo thundering in the heavenly sky.

It is they, who spit and curse,
Slander holy saints on the sly,
No other alters the pictures in the Bible
Treacherous they trip their own followers,
Minor gods
Only pardon when they can.

Still Time

The sparkle in my eye I renounced for sand,
For bricks I sold my face,
My shadow I exchanged for land,
And took in dogs to pass the time.

Now I live in this quiet house,
This golden house of mine.
I open the door only to those
Who bring me fresh eggs,
And take away my trash.

I still have time to learn whether
I should stay or go.

One day I might tear down this fence,
Perhaps one day I might leave,
A new face will breathe with this house,
A new pair of glimmering eyes,
While only dogs remain.

I still have time to learn whether
I should stay or go.
I still have the time to learn
The ways of right and the forbidden,
Does the clouded sky hold the answer?

Grand Cage, Minor Cage

The new acquisition of the zoo
Has ascended the throne
In a cage across the street.

All separated and unemployed,
Unaccomplished and dispossessed,
Throw meat pieces and candy
To this crownless king of animals.

The zoo's grey-haired director
Beseeches the visitors
To acknowledge the lion his honor and championship.
He asks them to keep clean,
To step down to the bar,
So he can treat all who came
He affirms
In his nature kind and sweet.

Grand cage, minor cage,
Grand cage, minor cage,
Cage from the beginning.

His mane is an insult to us,
Humiliation to our gaze,
For even from his cage
He dares to jeer at us.
We need no kings,
For our name is Majority,
And whoever dares to linger on our path
He becomes the zoo's
New acquisition.

Grand cage, minor cage,
Grand cage, minor cage,
Cage to the end of the beginning.

Light The Day

Tonight I'll help draw down the mist to embrace the earth,
Righteously we'll sow it across the fields,
At last, tonight our voices will be heard,
When the stars' monopoly is broken.
Firefly, the sparkles anchored in our eyes,
Propel us ahead as long as you shine.

Tonight once again I'll sickle down the lawn,
The useless grass in front of my door.
I'll send a postcard to former classmates,
Treat waiters to a drink,
Just don't tell me
All the letters were unsealed by mistake,
And don't tell me
By next sunrise the truth must fade,
Do not be subdued by the rumour of haste.
Don't tell me
Not yet has the dawn taken over the night,
Be silent for the rest still lies dormant.

Tonight we'll light up the day,
Even the birds share their skies with us.
Should your star have died out long ago,
We'll kindle a tiny sparkle, lost, in your eye.

Tonight we'll draw down the mist to embrace the earth,
Righteously we'll sow it across the fields.
We'll rob the stars of their monopoly,
And light the sparkles in people's eyes.
Tonight and never again we'll sickle down the lawn,
The useless grass in front of our door,
Send affable postcards to our old school friends,
And to a drink we'll treat them all.

Who Is The One?

A morning halo touches down on the rooftops,
Long awake, the cranes sail across the misty waters.
Behind us clouds a trail of raging smoke,
For we do not wish to be forgotten,
Like those to the eyes invisible.
Intellect and wisdom we neglect,
We skip across torrential rivers.
It's the sober who seek to find a road
That's found by those insane and bold.

Glimmer eyes,
And a roar beneath our feet.
Our country hastens past,
And nothing can stop us
In pursuit of our dream.
Intellect and wisdom we neglect,
We skip across the torrential rivers.
The sober seek to find a road,
The road chosen by those insane and bold.

Who, I ask, who is the one?
Who, I ask, who will be going with us?

For People

1. voice

To venerate me zealously,
To sacrifice victims to my honor,
This world of blissful beauty
I drew up for the people.
Upon the humble and pure
I cast a ray of hope,
For the modest and docile,
I abound with grace,
For the people,
For the people.

2. voice

My sway lies in the world of fire,
Where burning smoke whirls.
For the proud and fearless
To my kingdom lead the hidden trails.
Like cold days into fervid dreams,
I'll turn your needs into sweets.
I shall lift you above the others,
With divine powers I shall bless you,
For the people,
For the people.

Goat-bearded clawed seducer in a veil of elegance,
An incessant voice of truth that thunders down from heaven.
Up above unfold the heights of sky blue,
Vertiginous to the eye.
Down below lurk the traps
Tempting and devilishly dark.
For the people,
For the people.

Turn Over, Turn Over

Where riffles of the River Mura
Entwine the hovering fog,
The whirlpools of beautiful power
Entice us into their depths.
Mighty roar
Fills me with a gloom desire,
Its sound captivating
My heart and my soul.

I am gnawed by a question,
That yields no answer;
Grey banks
Or the water?
One or the other,
Advise me, my dear,
How to escape
These dark forces of dubiety?

Mura River,
Do not hasten my days away,
Turn, turn over
Another stone or two,
Or three.

Silently, my love
Takes her bow,
And leaves me
Alone with the water.
Where the waves of the Mura
Scour its bed,
There is my body seized
By the whispering whirlpool.

Mura River,
Do not sweep my days away,
Turn, turn over
Another stone or two,
For in a couple of my years
We shall see each other again.
Mura River,
Do not sweep my days away,
Turn, turn over
Another stone or two,
Or three.

On a Morning as the Sun Strokes the Land

First ray rises from its slumber,
See, the light has broken mist over the waters.

When the last in darkness yields to black depths,
A hundred new hearts rejoice at the sun.

On a morning as the sun strokes the land,
And heads feel clear and light,
We all take off to follow our path.
On a morning as the sun strokes the land,
And the tears run dry,
On a morning when the sun embraces the land.

By the rusty old stove, as years ago,
Warm palms and hats on the cabinets,
We travel back to that old song
No longer sung, that now cleaves us
With laughter that drowns even thunder.

On a morning as the sun strokes the land,
And heads feel clear and light,
We all take off to follow our path.
On a morning as the sun strokes the land,
And the tears run dry,
On a morning when the sun embraces the land.

The Farewell Ashes

I open the window to shed the ashes one last time,
To hear the tread that carries you away.
To inspire the oblivion, to expire your scent,
To exhale you, banished out of my dreams,
To hear the steps that draw you into the night.

Can I hold onto anything or have you taken it all?
A vow of love, a life-long sunset,
Golden rings and letters, all photos gone with you,
A summer getaway for two and a slice of heaven?
Can I hold onto anything or will you rob me of it all?

A new day still knows time to spare,
A child's cry sunk silent into night.
My fingers clasp to the first memory,
Your red belt reminiscent of that glorious night.

I open the window to shed the ashes one last time,
To hear the tread that carries you away.
The last melody I'd carry
There where it once played only for us,
To hear the step that draws you into the night.

A new day still knows time to spare,
A child's cry sunk silent into night.
My fingers clasp to the first memory,
Your red belt reminiscent of that glorious night.

Blossom Grove

Narrow path winds across the blossom grove,
The scent of life billows through the air,
Reds and whites all around us,
With rosemary that gives strength,
It is all in bloom, it all agrees, as once before.

Warble and sprouting, the rhythm of the grove,
Everything celebrates its own existence,
But there at the end the path converses with sadness,
There is the blossom, puny blossom of farewell.

One step through the days and decades,
Only one breath from exclamation till infinity,
There at the end the path entwines with sadness,
I pick the blossom, puny blossom of farewell,
I take the blossom, puny floret of farewell.

Far From My Beginning

The picture is fading into a grey oblivion,
On it your forefathers, along with your smile.
Lacquered shoes, a new lace-trimmed frock,
An enticing scent of her cake,
Your mother, how slender, how beautiful.

Who is he who sits with you,
And the young woman who cradles you?
A tall building now ploughs this soil,
I feel the spirits of yesterday,
What a sweet-faced child you once were.

Far in the depths of my past,
Far in the distance
Dwells my beginning, my place of birth.

Dark blue descends over the hilltops,
I bring my chambers to light.
Once ardent in my eye,
The glitter has now vanished with years,
And the colour is ever more a stranger
To the picture.

Far into the depths of my past,
Now in the distance
Dwells my beginning, my place of birth.

Vertiginous From The Height

No more, this cannot be real.
My wings have melted with fear,
Never again shall I rise up upon them.
And never I am to learn
They are only paper dragons
That have, for decades, hung over me.

As my mother taught,
You cannot see it all from on high,
And never are you to learn,
They are only paper smiles,
That have laughed, for decades, with you.

Vertiginous from the height.
Let the palm of your hand shelter me.
Your palm, soft and warm.
Let me come over to your side,
Let me hide in the palm of your hand.
You can give me back that ticket tonight,
For all I want is to be seen with you.

I Am Not To Blame

Detained in solitude, for a short while put away,
Until the sky reveals its true colour.

Do you remember me no more?
Does my voice rhyme with yours no more?
How devoutly I used to sit on your knees,
Waved my flag,
And sang the songs of your conviction.

You have the wrong man.
For I am not to blame, for I bear no guilt.
Your sight can focus no more,
From veins now vapors your power.

Moor To Sea

A hollow day, grey with drowsy silence,
Even the morning crickets' clamor,
It would have been better,
Had it not risen upon us.

Past faces, streets sunk in melancholy,
Nothing but merchandise and shortfall of the heart.
Silence supped up the jests' voice,
Even the sky casts its devil upon us.

Mournful thoughts narrate the past,
Sense elusive,
The fleetingness,
Of us who stand in our own light.

But when I lay my eyes on you, my dear,
The sky unfolds swift as lightning,
As if I owned the deep blue heights,
My soul dances with prominence.

But when I lay my eyes on you, my dear,
The sky unfolds swift as lightning,
Across the hills and plains I reach to see,
From my land of moors to yours of seas.

If I Had You

The alluring crimson petals,
Fragrant with temptation,
Rise above the stabbing cold thorns
That pierce the heart of a nightingale.
Even the Mura River I'd conquer for you,
Deny my own name too,
Like the sweetblood suckling tick
I'd bury into your heart.

I'd make the day for you,
Count the sunsets and auroras for you,
Shower your palm with droplets of rain,
If I had you,
If I had you.

I'd cover each trace,
Dye up my hair,
Like an estranged lover,
I'd leap straight upon you.

I'd make the day for you,
Count the sunsets and auroras for you,
Shower your palm with droplets of rain,
If I had you.

Beginnings

A beginning to a beginning, nearly the same,
In one blossom a thousand colours interlaced,
First footmarks, first step,
First day turns the world.

Slowly we grow, outpass one another,
Stroke gently, bite with ferocity,
Yet we are sole, embraced by our shell.

First lonesome night runs longest,
To mother's eyes her child shines brightest.
Days and hours, years entwine us
And moments scatter into endlessness.

Principles, honor and pride
Lead us all on
Into biting each other's flesh,
Into each other's hair.

Then, wise and mature
Hand in hand we conquer each day,
With us begins
The counting of days.
Then, wise and ripe
Cheeks against soil we lie,
Where even joyfulness
Kneels to honor sadness.

The morning dew washed the day,
A dog stood here and there
Far away.
First lonesome night runs longest,
For firsts know no other way.

Your name still raves above our stormy seas,
Lifted by thick branches to vertiginous heights
Your name still echoes from white peaceful fields,
However, with you gone
Life doesn't end.

There In The Mist By The Mura River

The elders still remember
When the village was woven into one,
Even a stranger was welcome
To raise a glass with a word or two.

At times, when the sun sank deep
Up from vineyard hills into our moor,
The echo of dulcimer allied with air,
The hamlet and meadows caressed by its flare.

Four men you were often to meet,
Mustachioed faces, clung to violins,
Their hearts imbued with soul-stirring music.
And if you gave away a daughter or two
The fiddle and double bass sharpened your heels.

At times, when dusk covers the earth,
And southern breeze ruffles the hair,
Then you might hear them play, vivid with lore,
In misty air above the moor.

Across The Mura, Across The Drava

We could have made an ideal pair,
Graduates enriched, with boisterous children.
This too has its own charm,
I now know,
With loans and monthly installments.
You've always cast a shadow
Over the poor offerings with which life blessed us,
Here and there I feel
As though I were still a newborn child,
Warm cloth wrapped in a stork's motherly beak.

Across the Mura River, across the Drava,
Across the Sava River, up to the stormy sea.
Perhaps even across the blue ocean,
From rocking cradle to the immense sky.

We could have made an ideal pair
Of grey painted old men reminiscent of life.
And that forty years back, "Jumpin' Jack Flash,"
Your decades-old vinyl gift,
Skips in time still.

The last August, the summer has left,
The silver hair frames you ever more beautifully,
Half my being is you,
Half your being is me,
Half my desire is still to fly.

Across Mura River, across Drava,
Across Sava River, up to the stormy sea.
Perhaps even across the blue ocean,
From rocking cradle to the immense sky.

Tonight We Play For You

Dear Guests,
Tonight, as a thousand times,
And as never before,
We'll carry you away,
To a place where each memory is born,
To a place where time rushes no more,
Dear Guests,
Tonight we'll ignite the stage for you!

Dim stage light to celebrate wine, sin and love,
Bitter sweet memories, rejoicing and feasts,
Tonight we'll play to heartiness and laughter,
To happiness, new beginnings, and major keys.

To all, who flew in on wings light as a bird's,
Even life stood in your awe.
To you who breathe without the haziest notion
Of that loud child's joy lurking in your hearts.
Dear Guests,
Tonight we play for you!

Tonight old sentiments will revisit,
Memories that burn,
Once wrapped in wind by the olive trees,
Tonight jasmine will scent the air again.

To all, who beat the obscure gloomy paths,
Those windy white roads
That ripen your sorrow and sadness to laughter.
To you who know the song will die out last
Long before the waiter finds time for us,
Dear Guests,
Tonight we play for us all!

Tonight we honour wreaths, farewell and death,
Anniversaries, tart tears and grief,
We play her eyes and her voice,
Minor keys and chrysanthemums white.

We Could Fly Away

Hey, I've seen this before,
I've experienced that too,
Stood under your oak window,
And fostered my sour-sweet jealousy.

Who has stood against whom and where,
Who has enjoyed her charms?
All familiar faces,
Alone too long.

We could fly away into the star-stirred skies,
And seize our own dreams,
By their wings of freedom we could ascend
Far up into the infinite sky.

Rusty old resentment
Still strangles the heart.
Frowned shaded gaze
Steals away the placid dream once more.
Who has stood against whom and where,
Should anyone really care?
A thousand times ruminated and chewed on,
Life is too short.

We could fly away into the stirred skies,
And seize our own dreams,
On their wings of freedom we could ascend
Far up into the infinite sky.

Who Are You?

Though I wear many years,
It seems as though since yesterday
In one breath I traversed the earth.
I would wander ever more.

Who is he, who treats me to dinner,
Makes offerings from his table,
Who lights up, extinguishes the days,
Outpaces and draws out
These lives
Of ours and others?

Your painful world
Where ink blots out the stars, who are you?
Your world that teaches me
Of humility and fear, who are you?

Who is he, who alters
The brave into the humble,
Who dares to reach into my heart
To turn a naive thought sly?

What's left of the heart,
Of ailment and joy,
What's left of the world
Will sluice to this imitation of life.

Today In Minor Key

Today I sing in minor key,
I don't know
What's to blame.
As if a thick cloud of mist
Laid upon my heart,
As if the sun lost its glare,
As if I'm only drawn back to my past.

Back, where we counted the river's days,
To its branches, to your white palms,
In those backwaters your sigh still quivers,
Drawing me back to that river.

Softly sing to me, sing into my ear,
Let no one feel my melancholy.
Let no one hear the blues in my heart,
When staring at the sun all I see is darkness.

Today I sing in minor key,
I don't know
What's to blame.
As if my legs were entangled,
As if they couldn't find their path,
As if they know not
Where the days have gone.

Bosnian

As Bosnian is to Slovene
Slovene is to Austrian,
Austrian is to German,
German is to Swiss.

Swiss: guardians of the
Black dictators' gold.

Fall In Anger

This vicious Fall
The wind will clip cold and merciless.
When the sun sets, beasts rise from the earth,
And starlings scatter in the sky.

Tattle-tale school boys who once sat in the first row
Now show me the way.
God drinks only the finest vintages,
Which summon and bury all things.

And in the end the snow will come,
As it has for the last thousand years.

You've been gone so long,
You don't know what it's all for.
Now that Spring is no more,
And the leaves have yellowed.

You've been gone so long,
You don't know what it's all for,
Even the lowest creatures of the earth still show their horns.

Black Veil

Its moment is soon to strike,
The echo of its whisper whirls around me.
I rush to close the windows,
Rub my drowning eyes with disbelief,
For shortly it will embrace me, cold.
Its dire breath smothers me,
Its claws clutched around my neck,
It haunts the path before me.
I shut all the windows tight,
Rub my eyes a hundred times,
But be damned,
The black veil still waits beyond the pane.

Its moment is soon to strike,
Shortly it will embrace me, cold.

The ravenous fingers,
And breath at my face,
It creeps through my skin
To close, raven-black, around my heart.
I shut tight the windows,
But its glow leaks through the cracks,
Shortly it will embrace me, cold.

Abel And Cain

The shades have melted into night,
But sleep comes slowly
And when morning rears its head
They'll be lurking beside me once more.

Now your letter
Corrodes my dreamless sleep,
I treasure it under the pillow,
Sleepless as day breaks.

We were not meant to be
We were like Abel and Cain
Perhaps in the next world
Our wars will be elsewhere.

Take me with you
Woven into your thoughts.
Our dreams lashed there already,
Like the weathered-wooden mill, to the river.
Sometimes the earth shakes
Before it calms
Sometimes the white-skinned birch trees weep
Before pain.

We were not meant to be
We were like Abel and Cain
Perhaps in the next world
Our wars will be elsewhere.

Immigrant Song

Other-worldly children joined our school
For those precious days
When the circus overtook our village

They must have been Yugos
For they understood us.

They defended the goal and dribbled
In a foreign way.
Their cries were different,
They were a new sensation,
Worldly and poor,
First to draw attention.
We all wanted to sit with them
To learn a trick or two.
We were star-struck
For tomorrow they might attend a school in Maribor,
The next day in England perhaps,
Children wild and wise.

They brought us
Names of exotic ports of call,
Which we carefully scrawled
In our small, well-worn notebooks.
Smells of distance and unknown.
These bold, maroon-eyed carriers of the world,
Which waits for us
Somewhere.

At twelve, I met the circus kids once more.
I slept on their bunk bed,
In that miserable trailer.
My mother passed out as they found me

The next morning at five,
After a night-long search
Up and down the Mura River,
The firefighters, militiamen, and boatmen.

Sure,
When their loudspeakers played The Rolling Stones,
When last month they were in Madagascar,
And tomorrow they'll go to Maribor,
And then perhaps to England.
As the magician summoned someone up to the stage,
The whole arena from that little village next to Mura hid
  beneath their benches,
So Stanci and I volunteered to perform with them.
And the acrobat kept referring to me as
Young master!

She must have been a Yugo
For I understood her.

Years on at an Australian airport,
The cymbals – hundred pounds overweight –
Said the lady at the counter.
Where are you from?
From Slovenia,
Gosh, I skied in Kranjska Gora, she said,
How's Bled?
Her eyes lit up with glow.
No overweight,
No worries, it's not a problem at all,
Safe journey,
Good luck Slovenes!

She must have been a Yugo
For I understood her.

See, As The Train Winds On

Look out at the Veneto,
The train winds the grey fields,
Far away lies its destination,
Abroad in the bloomless land.
Faces dark and creased with pain,
Their wooden suitcases, cracked with drought,
Now held captive by the train's screaming whistle.
The steam engine robs them of a dream,
As it tumbles down the parallel path,
With night sinking deep around them.
In which land will they wake?
Where will new morning break?

The fields, green with tall swaying grass.
Fields of youth,
Land that once resounded with child's play,
Laughter and joyous tears,
Exiles from a land of happiness past.

Sadness meanders down the rail slats,
Away from home,
Away from Matajur,
Far away
Far.

For a loaf of bread, for two chocolate bars,
For a new home built of coal.
The train will wind them to a stop,
To a new life among strangers, miners of the unknown.

See as the train winds out of the Veneto,
Away, away into the unknown.
The fields, green with tall swaying grass,
Will I smell it again,
When,
Ever again?

New Newer Newest

Slowly, day by day
The choruses that you've sung for centuries disappear.

Slowly, day by day
The names that you've carried for centuries vanish.

But the old river takes its time
As it flows past us.

Behind the seeming power
The fictive gods
Swagger into the sky.

Under the overlooked light
The overlooked talents
Dissolve into darkness.

New, newer, newest,
Sings the chorus of our ravenous thoughts.
Cheap, cheaper, cheapest
Corrodes whatever innocence we had.

Forget-me-nots

By the lake, on the shore,
Forget-me-nots blossom once more,
Still peaceful and blue.

On the shore, in my heart
Now, vivid blue,
Remains only the memory.

And as air of death befalls the roses,
The darkness creeps across my eye.
Peaceful and blue.
Lay them on my soil,
Forget-me-nots.

Time Born For Two

With each sunset, at the end of each day,
In a mirror cracked with age,
I see my time fleet by,
Covering over the forgotten memories.

The boy's knife never ceased to glitter,
The military badge from the JLA,
Tickets to see Queen at Tivoli Hall.

That was the time born for two
Who found their way to the stars.
You see no darkness when you blossom,
God knows what song you're listening to now.

Today the song sounds more profound,
With each sun rise, all around,
In the mirror of my children.

It's never too late for two
To connect on their way to the stars.
You see no darkness when you blossom,
God knows what song you're listening to now.

The other day this character tells me,
Mister Kreslin, my mom adores you,
She says you're really a fine man,
And that you went to the same college,
That was the time when youth led the way,
And life has never been as beautiful as it was then.
Mister Kreslin,
What would you say about that?

Well, sure, those were good times,
As good as they are today,
But only then was she young and beautiful.
All that happened in the past
Seems more beautiful,
But in truth, everything rocks
As long as you rock.

The Road

Long winds the road from village to city,
Long flows the river from the first cry to the last sigh.
Scarred and pot-holed with yearning,
Snow-melt pools, desire and sobs,
Long as a wakeful night
Long is this road from somewhere to once.

There by the road rise skyscrapers and Masai,
Here by the river kneels a girl dressed in white.
She veiled my world with her soft palm,
She drew me down to her way of life.
Yesterday the world seemed an exclamation,
Now it is a shower of questions.

Take me, carry me into the world
To embrace the questions.
Take me, bring me back home
That I may reveal the answers,
About this road
About this river.

Long winds the road from city to city,
Long flows the river from man to man.
Scarred and pot-holed with yearning,
Snow-melt pools, desire and sobs,
Long as a wakeful night
Long is this road from somewhere to once.

Kingfisher

Just once more, spread your wings and
Sing to me of your love,
A rider of the wind,
Who gazes like Narcissus into the clear water.
Just once more, spread your wings and
Sing to me of my love,
Through mist caressed by the echoes of your song,
From the cusp of dusk until the light of dawn.

Every morning day rises above the waters,
Counts the victorious and the victims of night's dreams.
Above the waters the vertiginous world
Steals dreams
That you stirred within me.

Tell me just once more, milk-white water lily
In the cloudy waters,
That each of your blossoms will open
Eternally
For all those beloved we have lost.

Black Guitar

At every feast
In those early days of youth,
Our home resounded with song
Played by mustachioed Gypsies.
My father, too, swept the strings of that black guitar,
The one he had bought
With his first wages.

Do you still have that guitar, Sir?
Sir, do you still play that black guitar?
That, sir, was the greatest of all.

Years on,
When they would pass and reach out for a coin or two,
They'd ask him about the guitar.
Years on, as they stole away to the bar,
Far from their resting instruments,
Which enchanted the guests through the night.
Their women too,
As they knocked on our door,
To plead for our garments, tattered and worn,
Would ask, eyes gleaming:

Do you still have that guitar, Sir?
Sir, do you still play that black guitar?
That, sir, was the greatest of all.

Once in a while, when back at my home,
I empty a few glasses,
Embraced by the shade of our chestnut tree,
I drink with my friends,
Whose lives are still bound to that land.
Then, strings by the table,

The Gypsies would appear,
Play for us,
And ask once again,
With their childish eyes and voices deep and coarse:

Do you still have that guitar, Sir?
Sir, do you still play that black guitar?
That, sir, was the greatest of all,
Indeed, the greatest of all.

Thousand Years On

That night as we slipped away,
You showed me the path to the skies,
You gave me the strength,
With which hearts endow their beloved.
Is this too little, or is this all,
Is this asking too much, or am I wrong?

A thousand years on I'll still be here,
The sun will be my heart,
And one of a thousand stars across the night sky
Will shelter me beneath its name.

I long to sing, to echo,
I long to outrun my own mortality
To strip the wings of time
The only righteous ruler.

The precious fruit is harvested from me,
Poetry, my son, and a linden tree.
Yet now it calls, shielded by inexorability,
For my body as well as my soul.

A thousand years on I'll still be here,
The sun will be my heart,
And one of a thousand stars across the night sky
Will shelter me beneath its name.

And tomorrow will rise once more
Dressed in the colours of yesterday,
And what befell us will befall.

A thousand years on I'll still be here,
The sun will be my heart,
And one of a thousand stars across the night sky
Will shelter me beneath its name.

Day Melts

Day melts away into crimson laced clouds,
As early as tomorrow it will break on a new horizon.
Day will draw dawn into a new kingdom,
And happiness, now dormant,
Awaits only the rising sun and waking eyes.

Would you be the same once more with the same souls?
Would you be you again among others?
Would you change anything, add something,
Lend your smile to more people?
I'd stop and scent the blossoms.

Take me there, where they still smile,
Where tear-strewn faces cry out loud,
Take me there, where slow paced songs play as if they
    had all the time in the world.

Day melts away decked in crimson lace clothes,
As early as tomorrow it will wake to a new horizon.
Day will draw dawn into a younger kingdom,
And joy, now slumbering,
Awaits the wake of children and men.

Instead of Whom Does the Flower Bloom

On a night when I share the vast skies with the storks,
Beneath the floating screen of haze,
Alone and silent, I mingle with them,
Feet upon the rain-scented grass.

As the first sunbeam eats through the dark,
We are drawn from the pool of our dreams,
And new desires, once tied to the sheltering moor,
Now vanish, as they sail into the heavenly blue.

Instead of whom does the flower bloom,
Instead of whom does my heart pound,
What skin smells sweetest of all,
And what song needs my voice to strike the stars.

Should the grasses bloom above me,
Some eyes will melt in tears,
While others will see only a flower.

Instead of whom does the flower bloom,
Instead of whom does my heart pound,
What skin smells sweetest of all,
And what song calls for my voice.

PRAISE FOR VLADO KRESLIN'S POETRY

"Legendary..."

– Michael Stipe of R.E.M.

"A major Balkan folk figure."

– Harvey Goldblatt, Head of Department of Slavic Studies, Yale University

"Vlado Kreslin is one of the greatest poets and singers from Eastern Europe ... His gentle soul and his powerful voice became a Slovenian national treasure ... His poetry moves high intellectuals as much as ordinary people ... I am simply in love with his music and his outstanding performances ..."

– Rade Serbedžija, Actor and Musician

"Marvelous ... [Kreslin provides] a magic fusion of so many Mitteleuropean motifs that put me in mind of everything from the films of Emir Kusturica to the novels of Bohumil Hrabal ... [Kreslin is] of such standing that everyone who comes to central Europe, from Dylan to R.E.M., plays with him ... So much great modern art and writing has risen out of the polyglot world of central Europe ... I realize that Kreslin's music is entirely of his own world, and yet enlarged that world to include anyone who wished to be a part of it."

– Richard Flanagan, Best-Selling Author of Gould's Book of Fish

"Kreslin is the Bob Dylan of the Balkans, a poet/troubadour of a lost Europe whose poetry, beautifully translated here into English for the first time, evokes a gorgeous and shadow-covered corner of Europe."

— *Noah Charney, Professor of Art History, American University of Rome, and Best-Selling Author of* Stealing the Mystic Lamb: the True Story of the World's Most Coveted Masterpiece

"Vlado Kreslin's *Instead of Whom Does the Flower Bloom* is a lyrical experience of beauty and longing. His moving and memorable poems remind us that we are all exiles, populated by fragments and longing for connection. An attentive, quiet mixture of the political and the personal, Kreslin's work summons the ghosts of all that has disappeared from our lives, and thus reminds us how the imagery remaining after those disappearances potently guides our memory and our history. How fortunate that *Instead of Whom Does the Flower Bloom*, artfully translated by Urška Charney, is now available to English speaking audiences."

— *Michael Sofranko, Poet and Professor of English, Houston Community College*

"Vlado Kreslin wrote some of my poems."

— *Miljenko Jergović, Bosnian Poet and Literary Critic*

BY AVAILABLE LIGHT

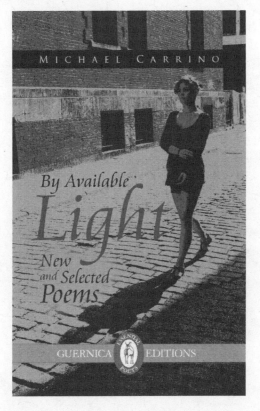

By Available Light is an education on how lost time can be recovered through poetry, how the murky, clogged waters of the past can be clarified by words and made to flow again. This book brings together the voices of son, brother, soldier, lover, traveller, and, as each one shares intimate stories, we are reminded that the poet is always more than one person, that he is all the lives and autobiographies his imagination can salvage. Michael Carrino's work is immediate and totally captivating, and he never writes without his two collaborators: heart and mind.

– *Luciano Iacobelli, author of* The Angel Notebook.

MIX
Paper from
responsible sources
FSC® C100212

Printed in July 2012
by Gauvin Press,
Gatineau, Québec